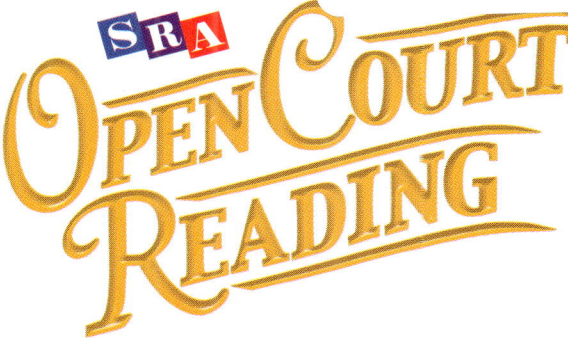

Beach
Peach

A Division of The McGraw·Hill Companies

Columbus, Ohio

www.sra4kids.com

SRA/McGraw-Hill

A Division of The **McGraw·Hill** *Companies*

Send all inquiries to:
SRA/McGraw-Hill
8787 Orion Place
Columbus, OH 43240-4027

ISBN 0-07-569935-4
    3 4 5 6 7 8 9 DBH 05 04 03 02

Peach

"Today is the best day I've ever seen!" said Pete.
He skipped past a peach tree. Then he stopped.
"Help! Help me, please!"
Who was asking for help?

"I'm here!" said a peach. "I seem to have
dropped from the tree. Can you help me?"

Pete looked at the tree. "I'm scared of being up
in trees," said Pete.

"Oh," said the peach sadly. "What will I do?" The peach began to weep.

"Can you play catch? Can you run on the beach? Can you make things with mud?" asked Pete.

"I can!" said the peach.

"Then come with me!" said Pete.

Pete and Peach had lots of fun.
They played catch.
They made heaps of mud shapes.
When it rained, they drew ships at sea.

6

Some days they would have a seat under a tree. There they would speak of the sea and the beach. They would hear birds peep and tweet.

Beach

One day, Mom said, "Let's go to the beach!"
Pete and Peach played in the sand.
They swam in the waves.

Then Mom said, "Let's take a rest!"

"Stay on the sheet," Pete said. "It is easy for a wave to sweep you off the beach."

Then Pete went to sleep, but Peach did not. He gazed at the sea.

"I will get Pete a special treat," said Peach to himself.

Peach went on the sandy beach. He looked at
seashells until he saw one he liked. It was a
pretty, pale green. It would make the perfect
gift for Pete.

Peach picked up the seashell.
Then a wave picked up Peach!

Pete saw that Peach was gone.

"Peach! Peach!" yelled Pete. "Where can he be?"

"Here I am! I am on this piece of rock!" said Peach.

Peach was not in reach!
"Jump to me!" said Pete.
"Will you catch me?" asked Peach.
"I will catch you!" said Pete. "Believe me."
Peach leaped into the hands of Pete.

"You must not leave when I ask you to stay," said Pete.

"I will not leave," said Peach. "But I needed a gift for you. It was a pretty, green seashell. But I lost it."

"That's okay," said Pete. "I'm just glad you are safe."

Later Peach said to Pete, "Thank you for saving me. What can I do for you?"

"You play catch. You run on the beach. You make things with mud," said Pete. "You are my pal, and that is okay with me."

"You are my pal, too," said Peach.
And then they went to sleep.